BREATH, BOOM

BY KIA CORTHRON

★

DRAMATISTS
PLAY SERVICE
INC.

2

BREATH, BOOM was produced by the Royal Court Theatre (Ian Rickson, Artistic Director; Vikki Heywood, Executive Director) in London, England, on February 21, 2000. It was directed by Gemma Bodinetz; the set and costume design were by Laura Hopkins; the lighting design was by Jenny Kagan; the sound design was by Paul Arditti; and the production stage managers were Debbie Green and Julie Derevycka. The cast was as follows:

PRIX .... Diane Parish
ANGEL/CORRECTIONS OFFICER .... Michele Austin
MALIKA/SOCKS .... Martina Laird
COMET .... Rakie Ayola
JEROME .... Howard Sadler
MOTHER .... Adjoa Andoh
CORRECTION OFFICER/OFFICER
DRAY/FUEGO/DENISE .... Amelia Lowdell
CORRECTION OFFICER/
SHONDRA/PEPPER/JO .... Kim Oliver
CAT/GIRL/JO'S FRIEND .... Marsha Thomason
JUPITER .... Petra Letang

BREATH, BOOM was produced by Playwrights Horizons (Tim Sanford, Artistic Director; Leslie Marcus, Managing Director) in New York City on May 31, 2001. It was directed by Marion McClinton; the set and lighting design were by Michael Philippi; the costume design was by Katherine Roth; the sound design was by Ken Travis; and the production stage manager was Jane Pole. The cast was as follows:

PRIX .... Yvette Ganier
ANGEL .... Rosalyn Coleman
MALIKA/SOCKS .... Kalimi A. Baxter
COMET .... Heather Alicia Simms
JEROME .... Russell Andrews
MOTHER .... Caroline Stefanie Clay
FUEGO/DENISE .... Abigail López
SHONDRA/PEPPER/JO .... Dena Atlantic
CAT/GIRL/JO'S FRIEND .... Donna Duplantier
JUPITER .... Pascale Armand

3

CHARACTERS

PRIX ("Pree"), 16, 17, 24, 29, 30

ANGEL, 16, 30

MALIKA/SOCKS, around 17, around 30 looking considerably older

COMET, 18, 26, 32

JEROME, 30s

PRIX'S MOTHER, 30s, 50s

3 C.O.s (Corrections Officers)

CAT, 15

OFFICER DRAY

SHONDRA, teens

FUEGO, teens

DENISE, 30s

PEPPER, 16 or 17

A GIRL, 16 or 17

JUPITER, 14

JO, around 30

JO'S FRIEND, around 30

All female except Jerome.

PLACE

The Bronx, New York City.

TIME

1986 – 2000.

BREATH, BOOM

ACT ONE

Scene 1

Street corner. Prix, Angel and Malika wait. Comet enters, pissed. She stares at them, particularly at Prix. They stare at her.

COMET. *What. (She waits for them to answer. They don't.)* Attitude? Don't even gimme that shit I *told* ju this is my birthday I'd appreciate the night off *please*, Toldju tonight my eighteenth big party *Ring!* Shit! Get the phone. I gotta leave my guests "Where ya goin'?" she says. "Stuff I gotta do" and you *know* she throwin' a fit, money she put out for that damn party "*I* know where you goin'! *I* know where you goin'! Huzzy!" Ain't that a sweet way talk to your daughter only daughter her eighteenth I think but say nothin', no time to bitch with her cuz I got the damn call, know my duty I come on down here and now yaw got nothin' to say? Hop my ass down to work cuz I'm called *my* birthday, *my* eighteenth birthday, leave my friends cuz *I* got a few, desert my *friends* to meet my *sisters* and now my sisters givin' me a look like why I got attitude. *(She waits for them to answer. They don't.)* What? *(Prix gives Angel and Malika a look. Comet is suddenly terrified but before she can get away Angel and Malika pounce, beating the crap out of Comet: no mercy. Comet screaming. Eventually Prix herself throws in a few kicks or punches. Boom: Prix looks up. Colored fireworks lights are reflected upon the girls. Prix stands, walks downstage, mesmerized by the lights. She says something, not loud enough to be*

5

heard over the pummeling and the fireworks. When, a few moments later, Malika realizes Prix had spoken, she pauses in her violence and indicates for Angel also to halt.)
MALIKA. Whadju say?
PRIX. *(Focused on the fireworks, absently repeats:)* Don't kill her. *(Having stopped the fight, Malika and Angel are now aware of the fireworks. Stand, also captivated. Drawn toward Prix's area.)*
PRIX. What day's today?
ANGEL. I dunno. Memorial Day? *(Prix, Angel and Malika continue gazing. On the ground behind: a bleeding, near-unconscious Comet.)*

Scene 2

Prix's bedroom. On the wall are several colored-pencil drawings of fireworks. Before the phone finishes the first ring, Prix snatches the receiver.

PRIX. Yeah? *(Prix has a pencil and pad and takes notes on the conversation. Angel and Malika on the bed, Angel weaving long braids into Malika's hair.)*
MALIKA. I don't know why Prix don't get a cell, always gotta make sure she be by her phone the right time, or by the pay phone right time. She have a cell phone she take her business with her, convenient.
ANGEL. She got a beeper.
MALIKA. *So?* People prefer a cell phone, beeper — you got the delayed action, gotta call 'em, push your number in, then wait 'til *they* find a quarter, they find a pay phone, then probably they gotta stand on line for the pay phone you know what kinda time gap that makes? Beeper, 'less it life-and-death vital, people say forget it.
ANGEL. Just why she say she got a beeper, she say beeper encourage 'em thus: "'Less it life-and-death vital, don't bother me" Girl! I hope you know these hairs is three shades lighter 'n your natural color.

MALIKA. They's highlights, J.W. likes it Ow!

ANGEL. J.W., J.W., you know how to have a conversation without havin' to plug your damn boyfriend's name every two seconds?

MALIKA. Last night he bought me roses off the street and stuck one in my hair. It was real sweet 'til that thorn stabbed my scalp Ow! I punched him and he punched me, then he goes ain't you just like Jesus, crown a thorns and we laughed and had sex and cookie-dough ice cream OW!

ANGEL. Toldju I do it professional, professional hurts.

MALIKA. Wow. *(She's looking around.)* Somehow I imagined Prix's room be all black, no windows. You ever been here before?

ANGEL. She's my cousin.

MALIKA. You ever been here before?

ANGEL. Yeah I been here before. Too many times, one buildin' away, too far for my mother get off her butt and walk but close enough she send me errand-runnin' every five minutes, "Aunt Kerstine, Mom's done with this week's *Jet*, said you wanna read it." "Aunt Kerstine, my mother like to buy couple food stamps, you got some extra?"

MALIKA. Your mom's nice. Soft. Not hollerin' all the time I bet she never even whipped yaw.

ANGEL. Kiddin'? One time Darryl and me ate the cream out the Oreos, hid the hard dark part in the couch —

PRIX. Okay. *(Hangs up.)* Meet at McDonald's ten thirty-five. Car'll come by ten forty-five, their party's a hundred forty-first, they established a dumb routine habit a saunterin' in between eleven-thirty and midnight. Cruise St. Ann's, round the block. First sight a their car, hit and get out.

MALIKA. A'ight. Ow!

ANGEL. You got dandruff like nobody's business, what kinda shampoo you use?

MALIKA. *(Wall drawings:)* I like your fireworks, Prix.

PRIX. Thanks.

MALIKA. My cousin rides planes sometimes. She does ... I dunno, secretary, somethin', she wears a suit, she has business other cities, gotta take planes. She says they bring food to ya. Snack and a meal. She says them stewardesses get free flights, Spain. Africa. That's gonna be me, stewardess. High, high, winkin'

7

down atcha from 37,000. *(Phone rings. Prix snatches it.)*
PRIX. Yeah? *(Realizing who it is, Prix looks at Angel and Malika, irritated. They are puzzled.)* Yeah. *(Hangs up.)* Someone buzz her in. *(Goes to her desk.)*
MALIKA. Who is it? *(Prix doesn't answer. Pulls from her desk various multicolored pipe-cleaner figures shaped like fireworks. After a moment, Angel interprets the silence:)*
ANGEL. Comet.
MALIKA. *Comet?* I thought she was still in the hospital.
ANGEL. *(Shrugs.)* Who else made her mad lately? *("Her" meaning Prix.)*
MALIKA. Who's mad at the people we're s'posed to hit tonight?
ANGEL. Not her she just followin' instructions. Nothin' personal anyway, just a drive-by, not like we shootin' anybody face-to-face. Get it. *(Malika gets up but, before she gets to the buzzer — in the hallway outside Prix's room — a knock is heard on Prix's door.)*
MALIKA. How she get in the buildin' without buzzin'? *(Comet opens the door, stands in the doorway. From the hallway: the sound of laughter, a man and a woman. Prix, molding pipe cleaners into fireworks, looks up toward the door.)* How you get in the buildin' without buzzin'?
COMET. Prix's moms and Jerome let me in.
PRIX. *(Turning back to her project, to herself:)* Fuck.
MALIKA. *(Vague smirk.)* I thought you were still in the hospital, Comet.
COMET. *(Entering, nervous.)* Got out. Coupla days. Hi, Prix.
ANGEL. How's Jupiter?
COMET. Good! Missed me. Only two but she got a vocabulary, my mother say "Every day that brat cryin' 'I want my mommy!'"
ANGEL. You gettin' along better with your mother? *(Comet looks at her.)* Leavin' her to babysit while you's in the hospital.
COMET. Who else?
MALIKA. She give you that big birthday party ain't that a new thing? Generosity?
COMET. Mother a the year.
ANGEL. She was ... Your mother ... while you was in the hospital, all by herself she was babysittin' —
COMET. First bruise I'da found on my baby I'da killed that

8

bitch. And she knew I was serious cuz when I come home first thing I inspect my daughter head to toe. Knew I meant it. Not even diaper rash. *(Pause.)* Angel. Show me?

MALIKA. You ain't got it *yet*? *(Angel falls back on the bed laughing.)* Aintchu practiced?

COMET. Practice all the time! just ... if I see her do it once more ... Angel?

ANGEL. *(Enjoying it.)* I dunno.

COMET. Come on.

MALIKA. Please Please Please Please!

COMET. I didn't say that! I just ... *(She pulls a razor blade from her pocket.)* If I watch just one more time —

ANGEL. Okay. *(Angel takes the blade from Comet, puts it in her own mouth, twirls it around her mouth expertly, periodically flicking it on her tongue. Eventually takes it out, hands it back to Comet.)*

COMET. God, I ain't never gonna be that good!

MALIKA. I can do it. Watch. *(Reaches for the razor.)*

COMET. *(To Angel:)* I lost so much blood tryin' it, I do it in fronta the bathroom mirror.

ANGEL. I lost blood too, at first. Your tongue gotta develop a crust.

MALIKA. You gotta keep practicin'. J.W. says I'm totally sexy when I do it, watch. *(Reaches for the razor.)*

COMET. *(To Angel:)* Practice any more I won't have a drop left. Watch.

PRIX. *(Not looking up.)* I find a spot a blood on my floor the owner's gonna lose six pints more. *(Comet, who had started to put the blade into her mouth, doesn't. Offstage voices:)*

JEROME. What did you say?!

MOTHER. I didn't say nothin'! I didn't say nothin'! *(A bang, as if someone had been thrown against the wall. Prix doesn't look up. A beat after the bang, then she speaks:)*

PRIX. Yaw stayin' all night? *(Angel and Malika get up, Comet was never sitting.)* Don't be late, Malika.

MALIKA. Why you always sayin' me? I guess Angel ain't never been late, why you gotta — ?

PRIX. Don't be late, Malika. *(Comet is looking at Malika and Angel.)*

ANGEL. Drive-by. McDonald's. Ten-thirty.

MALIKA. You don't have to worry about me I'm starved. I'll

bring J.W. for a bite ten o'clock, by ten-thirty I figure I be lip-smackin' Big Mac juice.

PRIX. Comet, stay. *(Malika and Angel exit. Prix still hasn't looked up from her activity. Comet observes the room.)*

COMET. *(Looking around.)* You sure like the fireworks.

PRIX. Everybody likes the fireworks. *(Offstage: a few moments of laughter and sexual breathing, which irritates Prix. After it quiets:)* "I'm gonna be eighteen, they catch me doin' what I'm doin' when I'm eighteen they put me away for life I'm quittin'! I'm quittin' the gangs When my birthday comes I'm gone! Ain't a damn thing they can do about it!" I be eighteen myself two years and liar if I say it ain't crost my own mind, ain't a dumb idea. Mouthin' off about it was. Ways you coulda fucked up, got yourself thrown out. We'd a kicked your ass and give ya the big punishment: you're gone. Now, stupid, gotcher ass kicked and here's the big punishment: you stay. *(Prix goes back to her pipe-cleaner figures. Quiet a few moments. Comet mumbles something, then glances at Prix, waiting for Prix to ask her to repeat. Prix doesn't.)*

COMET. I *said*, I thought we ain't s'posed to hit on our own, thought we only s'posed to spill blood a enemies. Or strangers.

PRIX. *(Dry.)* Yeah, we ain't s'posed to. See how low you brung us. *(Beat.)* Dontchu know better than to walk into a deserted narrow place, your sisters jus' waitin' for ya? *(Quiet again.)*

COMET. Whatchu wanna do? Shoot 'em off?

PRIX. Design 'em. *(Works quietly. Then:)* And shoot 'em off. Fireworks people ain't a architect, make the blueprint and give to someone else to build. Clothes designer never touch a sewin' machine. A fireworks artist, take your basic chrysanthemum, not to be confused with peonies, the latter comprised a dots but chrysanthemums with petal tails, the big flower, start with a pistil of orange then move out into blue, blue which comes from copper or chlorine, cool blue burstin' out from orange pistil, blue instantly change to strontium nitrate red to sodium yellow, cool to warm, warmer and the designer ain't the joyful bystander, she's right there pushin' the buttons and while the crowd's oohin' aahin' this'n she's already on to the next button. This quick chrysanthemum I'd start my show with and accompanying reports of course, bang bang and I'll throw in a few willows, slower timin' and a softer feelin', tension to relaxation keep the audience excited, antici-patin', then time for multiple-breakers, shell breakin' into a flower breakin' 'to another flower 'to another, then a few comets *(Points to drawing on the wall; refers to Comet:)* Comets! Then, *then* if I had a bridge, a *Niagara,* fallin' from the edge and this wouldn't even be the finale, maybe … maybe … somethin' gooey, like "Happy Birthday Comet!" *Now* finale, which of course is the bombs and the bombs and the bombs and "chaos" can't possibly be the description cuz this be the most precisely planned chaos you ever saw! *Hanabi!* flowers of fire. My show people screamin' it, *"Hanabi! Hanabi!" (Offstage:)*

JEROME. Bitch, where is it? *(Slap.)*

MOTHER. I ain't got it!

JEROME. You think I'm stupid?

MOTHER. *(Mocking:)* "You think I'm stupid?" *(A brief struggle with furniture banging. Comet continues admiring the fireworks art. Prix, vaguely embarrassed by her preceding enthusiasm, turns back to her project.)*

COMET. Sounds like my parents.

PRIX. He ain't my father. *(The offstage noise quiets. Not looking up:)* This stuff gimme a sensa shape. But sometimes I need the fire. *(Prix turns on her desk lamp, switches off the overhead lights. Pulls several pen lights out of her drawer, clicks them on. The bulbs are different colors. She begins moving them around, making different fireworks shapes and sounds. Comet smiles. Suddenly big offstage banging and arguing, screaming.)*

COMET. This fireworks finale I know too well. 'Bye. *(Exits. Prix goes back to her work. The battle rages on. A huge crash, then silence. Prix continues working. Eventually:)*

MOTHER. *(Outside door:)* Prix? *(No answer. Mother opens the door, letting herself in, and shuts it behind her. She is bruised from the fight. Prix doesn't look up.)*

PRIX. Lock it. *(Mother does. Dry:)* Guess he didn't kill ya. *(Mother laughs nervously.)* You kill him?

MOTHER. No, no he's okay. That crash … I hardly hit him I think he's mostly passed out. Wine. Lots and lots and lotsa … *(Sudden defensiveness:)* You think I wanted it? I got the restrainin' order! I got it, fourteen years! Fourteen years *dumb!* Fourteen years

I been puttin' up with it, finally I wise up, restrainin' order, six months it been effect, how many times he been here that six months? Seven! And I called the police first four times, him bangin' the door down. Slow as they is, and Jerome skilled with a paper clip, no problem he pick the lock 'fore they come, *if* they come why bother?

PRIX. *(Still not looking up.)* Didn't have to pick the lock tonight.

MOTHER. He was outside when I come home, o*kay?* I didn't want him to come in. We was talkin' ... Think I wanted it? It gonna happen anyway, I know it, I know it while I'm talkin' even though he ain't said it, I ain't said it, gonna happen and if I ... if I let it happen, don't fight it, it don't go over so rough. If I enjoy it a little, don't feel so much like he made me. *(Beat.)* I gotta get out. 'Fore he wakes, you be okay, you ain't the one he's after. I'm gettin' out. *(Beat.)* You wanna come? *(Prix doesn't answer.)* I'm goin', you be okay. *(Mother's hand on doorknob.)* Keep the door locked. *(Mother unlocks door and starts to open. A toilet flush is heard. Mother panics, shuts door, locks. Loud whisper:)* Prix! *(Prix ignores her.)* Prix! *(Prix, pissed and glaring, turns to Mother. Mother indicates the closet.)* Can I — ?

JEROME. *(Off:)* Hey! *(Mother rushes into closet, shuts door.)*

PRIX. Smart. *(Prix sloppily kicks a large furniture piece in front of the door, then noisily throws open her window and slams it shut. Sits back down at her work.)*

JEROME. *(Outside door, jiggling doorknob:)* I hear you! Dontcha be hittin' the damn fire escape! *(A clicking sound in the doorknob. Then Jerome forces the door open against the furniture and enters. Immediately rushes to the window, throws it open and steps out. A few moments later he returns, shutting the window behind him. He also looks roughed up from the fight with Mother. Prix continues her activity, not looking at him. He's playing with his paper clip.)* Whadju do, push her out? *(Prix doesn't look up.)* Didn't notice her broken body writhin' on the ground so guess not. *(Jerome moves toward Prix.)* Wonder what we do 'til your mama get back. *(Jerome touches Prix sensually. At the first contact, Prix slams him against the closet door, surprising him, hurting him; takes a razor blade from her mouth and holds it against his throat.)*

PRIX. I ain't five no more. *(Prix goes back to sit with her pipe cleaners, her back to Jerome. Stunned, he moves toward the door and exits. The outside door to the apartment opening and slamming shut. A few seconds of quiet, then the closet door is cracked open. Quiet weeping from inside. Eventually:)* If you weren't always playin' Helen Keller, bitch, you mighta knowed a long time ago. *(The quiet weeping continues.)*

Scene 3

Institutional waiting room. Angel sits glue-sticking newspaper clippings into a scrapbook. Prix enters. She is startled to see Angel. Angel sees Prix.

ANGEL. Whatchu doin' here? *(Prix continues staring at Angel. As Angel chatters she continues working on her scrapbook.)* Oh that's right, you got a mother in, since no one but me and my mother ever visited her I forgot. Ain't seein' her today though, Ramey *and* Sonia in Fuckers! I come all the way out here LOCKDOWN! And Ramey's section's the lockdownest, by the time they let him go visitin' time's almost over. *And* all he wants to do five minutes we got is bitch bitch bitch, jail sucks, no shit? But how 'bout just one "Nice to see ya" to his girlfriend trekked all the way out here, hour and a half subway and bus, think he appreciate that. And I tell him too, then he wants to get pissed, *I* ain't understandin', shit. If the dumb-ass hadn't been hangin' with Carl I *told* him 'at greedy punk get him in trouble one day! Three outa four cash registers they cleared and the idiot waitin' around cuz Carl can't bear to leave the fourth untouched. While he's clearin' it, guess what? *(Makes a siren sound.)*
PRIX. This ain't the men's side.
ANGEL. Seein' my sister, toldja Sonia in too. *(Prix glances at Angel's book.)* Scrapbook. Thought Sonia like to see it. Was gonna show it to Ramey 'til he pissed me off. Wanna see it? *(Prix shakes her head no. Angel looks at her.)* Your P.O. make you come? *(Prix nods.)* Glad I ain't been caught yet, no Probation Officer slave-masterin' my life.

Better go in, time's runnin' out. She know you here?

PRIX. P.O. told her. Probably just so P.O. can check on me after, see if I really come.

ANGEL. Better go. Time's runnin' out.

PRIX. What about you?

ANGEL. Forty-five minutes 'til they bring out the adolescents. But adult hour's now. She probably already there waitin' for ya. Go. *(Beat.)*

PRIX. You doin' that job? tomorrow?

ANGEL. Nope, takin' the day off.

PRIX. Off? *(Angel looks at her.)* Maybe you ain't got that choice, Angel — *(Angel indicates her watch. Prix reluctantly enters another space where Mother, who has been looking for Prix, sits at a table with a small partition that separates Mother from the other side. The partition comes about as high as the neck of a sitting adult. A Corrections Officer (C.O.) stands nearby. Prix enters. Mother sees her, smiles broad but nervous, not knowing what to say. Prix doesn't move momentarily, a decision: then walks over and flops down in the chair opposite Mother. Prix's body is turned to the side, away from Mother, and she does not look at her.)*

MOTHER. Surprise! They told me you was here but I didn't believe 'em. You look … You been eatin' right? Aunt BiBi tole me you been eatin' okay, I ast her to check on you now and again, she been by, right? *(No answer. Sing-song teasing a small child:)* I know what tomorrow is. *(No answer. Little more nervous:)* And your birthday next month, I ain't forgot nunna them holidays, I made somethin' for ya. *(Pulls them out. Prix doesn't look.)* Gloves! Hard to crochet 'em but … hope they fit … *(Mother reaches for Prix's hand. C.O. makes a loud, surprised grunt and snatches the gloves.)* Sorry! Sorry! You can check 'em before you give 'em to her. Her birthday comin' up, seventeen. *(To Prix:)* Took me nine weeks to do it. Just learnin'. *(C.O., who has inspected the gloves, holds them out to Prix. Prix, who hasn't budged a muscle or her gaze, does not look at C.O. C.O. shakes the gloves to get Prix's attention. Prix ignores C.O. C.O. lets gloves drop to the floor.)* When … When I get home I'm takin' you to Wave Hill. You never believed me, you think our neighborhood is all the Bronx is, uh uh. Bronx ain't just projects and bullets, there's parts got flowers, butterflies. Wave Hill, the

14

Botanic Gardens. The Mansion in the Park! when I get home, first thing we do is go to the pretty things, no! No, Thirty-Fourth Street, twelve midnight. You never believed me 'bout that neither, toldja midnight, Empire State Building, lights out ... *(Toward the end of Mother's speech Prix, without warning, has gotten up and exited, back to the waiting room. Prix sits in a seat near Angel. Angel still glue-sticking.)*
ANGEL. *(Not looking up.)* How'd it go? *(No answer. Angel doesn't notice.)* Wanna see my scrapbook? *(Angel opens the scrapbook. Prix pays scant attention. The book is filled with newspaper clippings. Pointing to various clippings:)* You remember Jeff Pace? Seventh grade, he made that environmental poster with the seals, won the contest? We was pretty good friends, I went to his funeral. Jeanine, remember? Too flirty. I knew she'd end up gettin' it cuz her home-boys always settin' her up to whore-spy on the enemy. She specifically requested her sexy pink dress, I know cuz she borrowed a piece a my notebook paper in U.S. History for her will, and here her mother laid her out like Sunday School. Tony, my ex-. You went to his funeral, right? *(Dancing a brief fast dance:)* His had the best music. Oh! this whole spread, centerfold *and* next eight pages, all my big brother, all Vince. His football stuff, honor roll stuff. "Athlete honor student killed by stray bullet." That's Terri, Trish's little sister. She was eight, she got it in the head, hopscotchin' when a drive-by come flyin' through, remember? Here's Lenny —
PRIX. You comin' tomorrow?
ANGEL. Pick your ears, Prix, I said no. *(Prix gets up to leave.)* Who the hell workin' tomorrow? Everybody want the day off. *(Prix heading for the door.)* You comin' to dinner? *(Prix stops.)*
PRIX. Toldja I got a job to do. Somebody got to.
ANGEL. *(Shrugs.)* My mother told me to ask you. *(Pause.)* Wonder how come she up and did it. Your moms. You know? *(Prix doesn't answer.)* Coulda done him in years ago. Why now? *(Beat.)* First degree. Betcha: twenty-five to life. *(Beat.)* You was two when she met him, right? And he with yaw all them years, you miss him?
PRIX. He wasn't my father.
ANGEL. My mom's gonna wonder why you ain't comin' to dinner, all alone tomorrow. Whatchu gonna eat?

PRIX. Egg rolls. Like every other night.

ANGEL. Okay, Prix. *(Her face back in her scrapbook.)* Merry Christmas. *(Prix exits. Angel turns the pages of her scrapbook one by one, absorbed and content.)*

Scene 4

Jail cell. Bunk cots. By the lower bunk, a couple new fireworks drawings. A chair. Prix and Cat in street clothes, Cat with a cloth band around her hair. Prix, in the chair, tears a page from a notebook she has just written on, stands to read. Cat listens.

PRIX. Six months ago a sense of personal injustice would have had me reaching for the trigger. Today I find my greatest defense is in open dialogue. It is the accepting, nonjudgmental atmosphere of my counseling group that has allowed me to reevaluate the choices I've made. Your support has opened me to revisit my mistakes and has helped me to see my errors as attributable to social and economic circumstances of my upbringing as well as to personal choice. My home was violent, my teachers suspicious, potential employers uninterested. Sometimes I think if I had been shown one kindness in my life, perhaps things could have been different. While I am naturally apprehensive about the consequential changes our group will undergo, I celebrate the release of three of you over the next several days, and welcome those newcomers who will be filling your seats. On this last day that we are one, my sisters, I joyously thank you for replenishing my soul and touching my heart. *(She has read seriously and continues silently looking at the page a few moments. Suddenly no longer able to contain it, she bursts into uncontrollable laughter. Cat follows suit.)*

CAT. "My sisters" "My sisters"! *(Prix's laughter subsides. She sits, erases on the paper, edits. No pause from previous speech.)* That's funny, you're smart. They eat up that crap, how long it take 'em figure it's shit? I like to see the look on their faces I'm comin' to your group tomorrow.

PRIX. *(Not looking up.)* You ain't in my group. *(Somewhere in Cat's following speech, Prix pulls out from under her cot a box of colored pencils and starts sketching. Will not look up.)*

CAT. I am now. I told Miss Collins I didn't feel comfortable in my group, she said Give it a try, you only been here a month, I said Some of them bitches threatenin' me, say they gonna take my teeth out. Randy. Scooter. She said I'll talk to 'em. I said I wish you wouldn't That really make life hell, I wish you just change my group please. The lie is, Randy and Scooter never said nothin' 'bout my teeth, I just hate their ugly faces wanted get away from 'em. The truth is, Miss Collins tell 'em what I said I *would* be in life-threatenin' trouble for lyin' 'bout 'em the first place. Luckily Miss Collins buy it I'm your group tomorrow. I like your group I like them people. *(Pause.)* Lap a luxury. Three meals. Street clothes.

PRIX. You the only one around here ready to print up the welcome travelers' brochure for jail. *(During Cat's following speech, Jerome will enter the cell, eyes on Prix. Prix sees him; Cat doesn't. He exits. Prix goes back to her sketching.)*

CAT. I hear 'em! Cryin' on the phone, "My honey, my honey," "I miss my friends." Most of 'em's honeys was kickin' the shit out of 'em daily and their *friends?* Their best girlfriend's on the outside and so's their honey guess what one plus one is equalin'? *(Beat.)* Could be worse. See them ugly green one-piece things they make the women wear? Least adolescents, we wear our own shit. *(Beat.)* Easy time. Five months you be eighteen, outa here, eleven left for me, shit. Scotfree both us and I'm fifteen, three more years a minor, I get caught, easy time. Eleven months I *know* my roof? *know* my mealtimes? shit. Damn sure beats the fosters.

PRIX. Usually all I hear's you whinin' 'bout the clothes situation.

CAT. Lacka choices! I *love* my clothes, but wearin' the same five outfits gets limitin' after awhile. There's this cute thing I useta wear, black, kinda sheer, kinda spare, my belly button on the open-air market. They say No way, Stupid! Their Nazi dress code, what. They think wearin' it'll get me pregnant? in *here? (Beat.)* Ain't my first time in. Fourth!

PRIX. Runaway.

CAT. Three more years I'm a fuckin' criminal for it! can't wait 'til eighteen! Runnin' away I be legal! *(Beat.)* My broken arm was mindin' its own business wisht they'da minded theirs, dontcha never believe that crap about best to tell the counselor tell the teacher it'll makes things better. Cuz ya *will* get sent back home and just when ya thought things could get no worse, they do.

PRIX. *Sh! (Prix moves against the wall. Someone is tapping against it, a code. Prix taps back in code. When the communication is complete, Prix sits back down to her sketching. Cat smiles.)*

CAT. What's the big one? Single most thing earned you all the gracious undivided esteem? I heard this: shot a enemy girl in the face. Then went to her funeral cuz yaw was best friends second grade, made all your sisters go, put the whole goddamn family on edge and every one of 'em knew and not a one of 'em said a word about it to you. *(Beat.) And* one time jumpin' a girl in, she not too conscious, you jump your whole weight on her face ten times maybe? twelve? 'fore a sister pull you off. *And* when yaw stand around, eenie meenie minie pick some herb comin' down the subway steps to steal their wallet, you was the one everybody know could always knock 'em out first punch. *And* one time on a revenge spree, dress up like a man so no one identify you later, stick your hair under a cap and shoot dead some boy years old. *And —*

PRIX. Fifteen. *(Pause: Cat is confused.)* I don't kill no kids. Fifteen.

CAT. O.G.! you gonna earn it. Original Gangsta, people respect you long after you retire Take me in! *(No answer.)* You get it. The high, right? This girl Aleea, she tell me all about it. The kickin' and smashin' and breakin' bones snap! Somebody lyin' still in a flood a their own blood, somebody dead it gets her all hyped up, thrill thing! And power, them dead you not, *you* made it happen! Them dead, *you* done it! You ever get that high?

PRIX. 'Course. *(During Cat's following speech, Jerome will enter. Prix takes Cat's hairband — Cat doesn't notice — and effortlessly strangles Jerome to death.)*

CAT. Take me in! I tried once, not yours. Not the other neither I ain't enemy! Small little club I was interested in. Wore the right colors, I talked the shit. They wouldn't even jump me in, I said "I'll do it! Either way, all yaw stand in a line and rough me through it OR I'll take the toughest one on, two minutes!" They just laugh.

(Beat.) Maybe when we out ... I know there's lots and lots a members, big network your group, maybe ... I'd be good! Runnin' with my sisters, tappin' the codes —
PRIX. *(Strangling:)* Wannabe. *(Prix back to her sketching. Jerome exits.)*
CAT. They think I ain't tough I got it! I can fight! I was four, these two boys was six, tried to steal my bike I flattened 'em! And when my foster sisters steak-knife stabbed me and drowned me in the tub, somebody called a ambulance, he mouth-to-mouthed me back alive, said if I wasn't strong I'da stayed dead. *(Chuckles.)* She's dead! Jessie, she the one screamin' "Hold her down! No air bubbles hold the bitch 'til she dead dead dead!" Look who's talkin', she with her homegirls and boys thinkin' she a member in good standin', got drunk one night and said somethin' smart to a homey, he blew her head off. *(Laughs.)*
PRIX. You ever wish you done it?
CAT. *(Beat.) Huh?*
PRIX. You ever ... You ever regret wasn't you pulled that trigger?
CAT. *(Confused.)* She's dead.
PRIX. Yeah but like ... that thought. Fantasy. It ever get stuck your mind? Wishin' the last thing she seen was you robbin' her last breath?
OFFICER DRAY. *(Off, yelling to someone else:)* You heard me, I said Move on!
CAT. Bitch! You know that ol' crackhead Tizzy? Officer Dray told me I was mouthin' off, I wa'n't doin' nothin'! She goes Move along and I do and she goes Don't roll your eyes at me! and I go I *moved* along and she goes Don't gimme nunna your lip! and I go *(What're-you-yelling-at-me-for? gesture)* and she goes Alright goddammit mop the floor with Tizzy! and I think Oh fuck but I do it, shit. And ol' Tizzy don't shut up, bitchin' all outa her head, and I go Oh shut up ya ol' crackhead bitch! And she goes, *(Suddenly struggling to contain laughter)* she goes, "Hey! One day you gonna be me!" *(Prix looks up, not at Cat. Cat is rolling on her bed, uncontrollable laughter.)*

Scene 5

Counseling room. Fuego and Shondra sit. Room is represented by four or five folding chairs, indicating that this is half of a larger circle of perhaps ten people.

SHONDRA. What makes me mad? What makes me mad is the shit they call food. Allow us no chocolate but meanwhile what *is* that cold fried shit they slop on our plates? Tater tots? What the shit is tater tots? What makes me mad is goddamn body searches before visits, after visits. What makes me goddamn mad is havin' to sit here talkin' shit and listen to all yaw talkin' shit when I don't give a goddamn and yaw don't give a goddamn, that's what makes me mad. *(Cat enters.)*

FUEGO. *(Indicating the "Counselor":)* I think she means what makes us mad on the outside.

CAT. Hi, Fuego. Hi, Shondra. *(Sits.)*

SHONDRA. *(Eyes on "Counselor":)* Hi. I *told* ju in individual counselin' why the shit I gotta be dredgin' up my business in fronta everybody.

FUEGO. So we can help each other. *(Breaks into laughter.)*

CAT. Missin' classes when there's a lockdown, that's what makes me mad.

FUEGO. Fuck ain't nunna these bitches I look to for help 'less I need help gettin' my throat slashed, there I find lotsa helpful friends.

SHONDRA. I got no friends. I got sisters. And associates.

CAT. The clothes make me mad. How come only five outfits?

SHONDRA. *(To Cat:)* I catch you lookin' at my stuff in the shower again I'ma mess you up.

CAT. I wa'n't lookin' at you!

SHONDRA. *(To "Counselor":)* Don't tell *me* this ain't the place for that! I see some bitch lookin' between my legs I'ma —

CAT. *(Mumbles.)* Like you two don't do it.

20

FUEGO. Whadju say?

SHONDRA. *(To Cat:)* Yeah, dontchu worry about it.

FUEGO. *(To Cat:)* Whadju say?

SHONDRA. She said she was fuckin' lookin' where it was nunna her uglyass business to be lookin'.

CAT. I saw ... I saw ...

SHONDRA. Stupid obviously don't understand the difference, wants and needs. I *need* a man's touch but none around, I take what I can get. But if you *look*in', Tom-peepin', that's cuz you *want*nit, you *want* a woman and you was probably doin' women out there

CAT. I wasn't!

SHONDRA. *(Uninterrupted:)* and tell ya somethin' else,

CAT.	SHONDRA.
I wasn't doin' it!	this be your one warnin'.
(Beat.) I WON'T DO IT	I ever catch you —
NO MORE!	

(Prix enters and sits. At first sight of her, Shondra and Fuego sit up straight, fall to silence. They don't look at her, or at each other. Cat had continued speaking until becoming aware of the sudden stillness. She is surprised by the fear-respect. Takes it in. Suddenly Cat's head turns, as if called on by the Counselor.)

CAT. Home? Mmmmm ... I guess ... the garbage. Makes me mad when the garbage gets piled high my street, the rats ... It ain't even a strike! If it was a strike I'd understand but regular thing, that high garbage, these rats —

FUEGO. I don't understand the damn system, I don't see how I can get charged nine felonies when they only caught me doin' two. *(New thought, looks at the Counselor:)* They gotta prove it. *(Waits momentarily for an answer; when none comes:)* They gotta prove it! right?

SHONDRA. Not respectin'. Cuz I been doin' it a long time, I got some experience. Then somebody, fourteen, fuck up the goddamn instructions, I get on her about it, she say, "I didn't forget the codes." I get on her about it, slam her head 'gainst the cement wall, "I didn't forget the codes." I slam it slam it slam it, "I didn't forget the codes." Last thing I hear some kinda mumble, "I didn't — " lyin' to the end out on the ground, out cold I kick her stupid stubborn face. All she had to do was admit it, shit. And if I'd killed the dumb bitch, guess *I*'d be the bad guy. *(A silence.)*

FUEGO.   My sister Enrica, she taught me backgammon, she's fifteen, I'm nine, we're still in Texas. Every time she roll double sixes, she go, "Boxcars! Boxcars! Lucky!" Then, one day Enrica suddenly all mean, screamin' all over the house, *loca!* And this bad mood don't pass. Hear me rollin' the backgammon dice, she come punchin' my face, Mami have to pull her off. Monday at school the girls giggle at me, "*Hermana* boxcar! *Hermana* boxcar!" Eventually tell me Enrica joined the gang, attached to a boy gang and new girls gotta roll in. They hand Enrica two dice. Boxcars, but this game boxcars is bad luck. Twelve of 'em. Toughest boy was engine. Littlest boy caboose. *(Beat.)* I like New York better. I like jumpin' in here, better 'n rollin' in, all I got from jumpin' in was a couple broken ribs they healed. *(Silence.)*

CAT.   *(Suddenly sobbing:)* They took 'em away! They took 'em away!

SHONDRA.   *What?*

CAT.   Little boy!

FUEGO.   What're you talkin' about?

CAT.   Had a baby! Little boy, they make me, they make me adopt him away!

FUEGO.   Can't no one make ya ya musta said yes.

CAT.   They said Do it! They said Do it!

SHONDRA.   Where was ya gonna put him? Get a double cell, one be the nursery?

CAT.   Before I was charged! I oughtn't be here no way, awaitin' trial, innocent 'til proven guilty, how come I gotta sit here for lacka five hundred?

FUEGO.   *Five hundred? (Cat looks at her.) Dollars? (Cat nods, confused.)* Not five hundred thousand.

CAT.   No!

FUEGO.   Fuck I wish *my* bond was fuckin' five hundred dollars I'm here 'til I come up with ten thousand here to eternity.

SHONDRA.   Depends on whatchu in for. Whatchu in for? *(Shondra knows. Cat, caught, scared, refuses to answer.)* Well let's see what could possibly be judged that puny bail. *(Shondra looking at Fuego. Feugo confused a moment, then gets it.)*

FUEGO.   *Prostitution?*

CAT. They ain't proved nothin' yet!

FUEGO. *Prostitution?*

CAT. FUCK YOU! like you any better!

FUEGO. *Hell*uva lot better I ain't never taken no money for it I ain't never been *that*.

SHONDRA. If ya took it for money you be a *(To Counselor:)* No, I *won't* shut up! If ya took it for money maybe ya still have a little dignity. Funky filthy on the street, whore been tradin' it for a Big Mac. *(Fuego roars in laughter.)*

CAT. AIN'T TRUE!

SHONDRA. Is and you know it, I know somebody goddamn bought the burger. *(To Counselor:) What?*

CAT. You'da done it too! you was hungry! You was hungry like I was —

FUEGO. I don't get that hungry.

CAT. You don't know! *(Shondra and Fuego laughing hard.)* FUCK YOU! YOU DON'T KNOW! *(Shondra and Fuego doubled over laughing. Cat turns her back away from them and from the audience. Freeze.)*

PRIX. *(In her head:)* What makes me mad is music. John Philip Souza, trombone pansy crap. And I *tried* Handel, shit he *wrote* for 'em but most of it's too damn obvious. Still, I go for the *1812* cliché. And my head's designed about seven rap shows, comets for the basic beat, butterflies and palm trees the chorus. Chrysanthemums ain't on any regular rhythm but rather hit the hardcore politicals: "power" and "fight" and "black black black"! But it's all stupid, first of all the differential between speed a sound and speed a light means music and visuals ain't never be lined up perfect like some goddamn video, and who *needs* it? Fireworks got their own music: reports and hummers, whistles. Magic, each one born with that little sound. A gulp. A breath. And we holdin' *our* breaths, waitin' three ... four ... five ... BOOM! And my *heart* boom boomin', the final moment of the finale bang! flash! *(Beat.)* Then nothin' left but pastel smoke, pink, blue floatin' calm. Calm.

Scene 6

Cell. As Cat chatters she will pull the sheet off the upper bunk, then sit tying it. She is cheery. Prix reads a tattered paperback black romance novel, does not look at Cat.

CAT. *(Admiration:)* You the coldest fish I know! Ruthless! People know it too, you walk into a room, silence! *(New idea:)* Prix. Come to my Geometry tomorrow. I like Geometry but those dumb bitches just come in bitchin', bitchin' interrupt the class then I don't learn nothin' but you walk in, everybody shut up, everybody know who you are, get quiet fast, come on, Geometry! I like that math. Circles is three sixty, a line goes on and on, rectangle versus the parallelogram, interestin'! Ain't fireworks geometry? Can't the study a angles and arcs be nothin' but helpful? Come on! Favor for me? *(Prix chuckles to herself. Cat, not necessarily expecting the refusal, is delighted by it.)* I know! you don't do favors! You the coldest fish I know! *(Beat.)* You met Ms. Bramer? She's the new Current Events she's nice I hope she stick around awhile. She say the six o'clock news always hypin': "Tough on teens! Youth violence outa hand, try 'em like adults!" But she say news never say three times as many murders committed by late-forties as by under-eighteens, Ms. Bramer say news never mention for every one violence committed by a under-eighteen, *three* violences committed by adults *to* under-eighteens. Ms. Bramer say if we violent where we learn it? Sow what you reap.
PRIX. Reap what you sow.
CAT. *(Having just noticed Prix's reading material.)* I know that book! passed to me months ago. She's a lawyer, pro bono, he's a big record producer. He's rich and she appreciates it but she don't know, loooves him but got that lawyer's degree and don't know she can lower herself to *that*. I didn't think you read that stuff, I love you and roses and wet eyes. *(Beat.)* You ever plan your funeral?
PRIX. Fireworks.

CAT. Knew it! Nothin' somber for me neither, I got the tunes all picked out, went through my CD collection I know who my special guest stars be, I figure they come, like this poor unfortunate fifteen-year-old girl died, ain't the city violent and sad? We feel so depressed we come give a free funeral concert, her last request. Good publicity for them. Here's the processional tune: *(She begins humming a lively hip hop piece. Interrupts herself.)* Processional, when the people first walks in with the casket. *(Resumes her humming. Stops.)* My coffin's gonna be open. Yours? *(Prix turns a page.)* I'm gonna look good, I got the dress picked and I want people to see it. You ever plan your suicide?

PRIX. Fifth grade.

CAT. Pills? Gun stuck up your mouth?

PRIX. Off the Brooklyn Bridge. *(Now puzzled:)* Would that kill ya?

CAT. World Trade Center better bet, know how many freefall floors to concrete? Hundred ten!

PRIX. Knew this girl, Emmarine. Eighth grade social studies. Her thirteenth birthday tried, fucked it up. Now she got little cuts on her wrists and everyone at school smirkin' wherever she walks. On her locker, someone spray-paint "Emmarine, Suicide Queen," like they ain't never thought of it themself, and someone else ex out "Queen," write over it "Flop."

CAT. You noticed I ain't been around last twenty-four? Infirmary, doctor checkin' me out after this girl come up to me *pow!* She say, "What your name?" I'm tryin' to answer, "My name's Cat" but before I get the first word out *pow!* She punch me in my face I'm all knocked out!

PRIX. Not any damn home sets I'm gettin' professional stuff, Class B pyrotechnics, the flowers and 'falls and rain takin' up the whole sky, in my will the details of this spectacular will be specified, my careful plannin' will reap the benefits: the audience mesmerizement, the big boom!

CAT. Supper tonight, I seen her people, them girls follows her around, she weren't there guess they threw her in the bean. I come to her girls, say, "Your friend ask me what my name is. My name's Cat." But soon as I say "Your friend ask me what my name is" they start laughin' so hard I think they don't hear the second part, so I keep sayin' it louder but the louder I say it the louder they laugh.

"My name is Cat!" (Giggles.) "MY NAME IS CAT!" *(Giggles, stands on the upper bunk.)*

PRIX. Most appropriate funeral finale cuz they wasn't just my life. My death. Tragic, someone gimme cotton socks, I *think*, Christmas present and I walk into the shop wearin' 'em. 'Cep' turns out they was silk. Static electricity, spark, boom! "God," they say, "how could this happen? To *her?* Always double-checkin' her clothing, she of all people." Scene a the unfortunate event, they note how I generously spaced apart each of my twenty-five fire-works houses so one accident is prevented from causin' a chain reaction and they'll wipe their wet cheeks, touched that I protect-ed others, touched I died alone. So young, so young. *(As Prix speaks, Cat has swung the sheet — tied into a rope — around an over-head horizontal pipe and secured it. It is suddenly clear that she has formed a noose. Standing on the edge of the bunk, she has stuck her head through it. If she jumps off, she'll hang. The cheeriness has van-ished. Her eyes are closed, her breathing harsh and uneven. The most delicate push would be enough to knock her over. Now Prix turns to Cat, looking at her for the first time in the scene. Though Prix has not been aware of Cat's activity, she does not look surprised.)* Jump. *(Blackout.)*

ACT TWO

Scene 1

Kitchen table. Prix and Jerome at opposite sides, he sipping coffee, she with a fast-food milkshake. On the table are a clock-radio, a gun, and many vials of crack that Prix silently counts, moving her lips. She will periodically glance at the time.

JEROME. Way I figure it, woulda made better sense I killed her. Statistically speaking, man kill his wife, whether from a argument whether he stalked her, crime a passion, three, four years tops. Woman kill her husband, response to him whoopin' the devil outa her decade or two, it's murder one, she get twenty-five to life. Seven years since she gimme the gun, she ain't yet served a third a the minimum time. Other way 'round, I'da been out, parta regular life four years now in the simple name a freedom, in the name a quality a human life, wouldn't me snuffin' her been the more logical choice, long run?
PRIX. You weren't her husband.
JEROME. Common law. Fourteen years we was together, common law husband —
PRIX. Shut up! you're mixin' me up.
JEROME. And common law father to you, man whose genes you got you never met. If your mama even know who that is so I'm the only father you ever ... *(Prix is looking at him.)* Okay! I wasn't the best daddy Who's perfect? Only said I was all the daddy you had. Maybe I wasn't around for *conception*, maybe I didn't *breathe* life into ya not there glimpse your first breath, but I was around pretty much all the breaths thereafter I think I had a impact, your life. Sometimes ... Sometimes your mama couldn't make the rent, I help her out a little. Once I remember her flat broke, I bought the shoes for ya.

27

PRIX. *(Flat:)* I don't remember that.

JEROME. Seven years old tap-dancin' the shoe store, new white buckle sandals.

PRIX. You lied your whole life now guess you gonna lie your whole death.

JEROME. I gave yaw money! I remember ... I remember helpin' with the groceries once —

PRIX. Shut up! *(Beat: Jerome picks up the gun, studies it.)*

JEROME. Your mama always found it such a curiosity, fireworks fixation. All make sense to me, one way or another you love the bang bangs.

PRIX. Chinese invention, they find a purpose: beautiful. Spiritual. Not 'til a English monk put his two cents in do white people decide gunpowder for killin'. *(The noisy end of the milkshake.)*

JEROME. Ain't that a healthy breakfast, chocolate shake. Hey. Thought you had to go out, big appointment.

PRIX. Gotta do the inventory some point. Long as I'm waitin' — *(Eyes on clock-radio:)* When the fuck — ?

JEROME. If you was smart you'da put your time inside to some kinda trainin', no need it have to be total waste but no. Your brain too much the street.

PRIX. Since they recently slashed the higher ed, I'm left with these options: specialize in shampoo, specialize in relaxers. I say I liketa specialize in Class B pyrotechnics. They say Ha ha, real like-ly they apprenticeship a felon with explosives.

JEROME. Boo hoo life so hard. Least you had counselin', school. I got nothin', dropped out and into the army, pulled in by the college promise, then they fine-print robbed me out of it. And the kinda job trainin' I got be real useful. Next time some country invade New York. Think I sit around woe-is-me? Always found somethin', *legal.* Street cleanin', janitor — *(Phone rings.)* One time — *(Prix makes a brief shush noise-gesture, glaring at him. Phone rings a second time, third. At the first sound of the fourth, she picks up. Lets the other person speak first.)*

PRIX. Oh, you.

JEROME. Maybe I wa'n't Daddy a the Year but I offered support, legal.

PRIX. *(Into receiver:)* I was hopin' it was them, you're late. Come up, I gotta go.

JEROME. What, you think you be up for the complementary daughter award? You sure ain't the gran' prize! Your own mama, seven years and you ain't writ, ain't seen her, not since that probation officer enforce ya, sixteen.

PRIX. I ain't got time, Comet.

JEROME. But then how couldja visit. Never bothered find out what prison she been moved to. Five years back. *(Prix hangs up, obviously cutting off Comet. Puts on jacket, takes gun back, pulls from jacket pocket a little notepad, studies.)* You ain't got that intercom fixed yet? All this time, still somebody gotta announce theyselves by the cross-the-street pay phone? Then you guess how long it take 'em get back across, buzz 'em in. *(Prix, paying no attention to Jerome, pushes the buzzer and holds it a few seconds.)* Lucky. So far. You ain't been to jail since that year in juvie, and your auntie move into your apartment, bigger 'n hers, hold it for ya 'til ya get back. Be there when ya get out, family company. But, released, your damn attitude drive her out after four months, get caught your business this time you be put away *years*, and who you think hold on to your home this time? No one! Gone! *(Knock at the door.)* Ain't twenty-four bit old still be playin' gang gal? *(Prix glances through the door peephole, begins undoing the various door locks.)* You goin' back. Lucky, you been kickin' all six years since you got outa teen hall and your blind parole police ain't suspected a thing, but sometime you goin' down, I got a prediction for your life: jail — second home. *(Prix, who'd finished unlocking, relatches a lock.)*

COMET. PRIX! *(Pounding.)*

JEROME. No, first.

PRIX. WAIT! *(Pounding stops. Prix walks to a closet.)* Here's a present. *(Prix takes out of the closet a cupcake with a candle that is obviously a stick of dynamite.)*

JEROME. *(Pleased.)* You remembered.

PRIX. I better let her in 'fore she breaks it down. You light the candle later. *(Jerome smiles and exits off the side of the stage opposite the outside door, which Prix opens. During Comet's following speech, the sudden reflection of various colored lights — fireworks — from the direction Jerome exited. Prix notices without expression. Comet doesn't notice.)*

COMET. *(Drops into a kitchen chair.)* Jesus givin' me all that shit

29

for bein' late then take ten minutes to open the goddamn door! And I *told*ju in the first place I might be five minutes delayed cuz my mother gotta come watch the baby I *do* have kids you know. And don't say Jupiter ten years old, I ain't one a them damn mothers turn her oldest into babysitter. And the baby teethin', hollerin' —

PRIX. Needja to answer the phone.

COMET. You called me over here for that? When you gettin' a fuckin' cell phone, Prix? *(Prix, looking over her notes, ignores Comet.)* Why me?

PRIX. Cuz you on the payroll.

COMET. Call me all the way over here —

PRIX. They left a message on the machine, I better be here eleven to eleven-thirty cuz they be callin', they leave no number for me to call back. Meanwhile I have another appointment, pickup I gotta do now. *(As Comet speaks, Prix pulls a backpack out of the closet, starts emptying it.)*

COMET. So fuckin' sicka this. Thought kids I'd give up the life. Welfare sure don't cut it. I gotta gangbang supplemental income for the luxuries: food. Diapers.

PRIX. Let it ring three times, *exactly three times.* The moment you hear the fourth ring start pick it up. Say nothin', they'll talk. Take notes. *(Tears relevant pages out, tosses rest of the pad to Comet.)* At the end they say "Got it?" you say "Got it." And you *have* it. *(Stares at Comet, no response.)* Okay?

COMET. O*kay!*

PRIX. I'll be back fast they may not even call by then. Right on the corner. Five minutes. *(Prix shuts the door behind her. Comet looks around, bored. Turns on the radio and searches 'til she finds a station she likes. Eventually the phone rings. Comet quickly turns off radio. Phone rings three times. Stops ringing. Comet is freaked, doesn't know what to do. Picks up receiver, quickly puts it back. Eventually phone begins ringing again. She is confused, panicked. As the third ring commences she snatches the receiver, listens. Gives a little cry.)*

COMET. Shit! Shit! Shit! Shit! Shit! *(She stares at the phone, crazy. Prix enters, sets her backpack down.)*

PRIX. They call? *(Comet doesn't answer. Prix looks at Comet.)*

COMET. THREE! rang three times and I was waitin' for the fourth but it STOPPED! God it STOPPED and I was scared I miscounted or they miscounted or they toldju wrong then it started ringin' again GOD! God Oh Jesus I thought Oh Jesus Should I pick up? should I — I did! I — I guess I was afraid it would stop ringin' again so I guess I picked it up picked it up too soon JESUS! Oh JESUS they hung up! I picked it up JESUS I'm SORRY, Prix! Jesus they hung up I'm sorry, Prix. *(Prix, seething, glares at Comet. Finally opens her mouth to speak but before any words come out, the phone rings again. They both stare at it. At the top of the fourth ring Prix snatches the receiver and the pad. Comet's entire body relieved. Prix jots down notes.)*

PRIX. Got it. *(Hangs up. Sits in the other chair, not looking at Comet. Thinking. Quiet.)*

COMET. Prix —

PRIX. 'Bye, Comet. *(Comet goes to the door. Opens it. Then suddenly turns to Prix.)*

COMET. I ain't just nothin', Prix! Know that's whatchu think soft, Soft Comet, still cries at movies still cries at funerals, I don't want it! I never asked to be boss, Prix! You act like I'm failin' at ambition, PRIX! I'M HERE! WHERE I WANNA BE I never asked for nothin' but a little stash to sell, just get me my kids by. I ain't got your leadership quality, Prix, don't name me worthless just cuz my personality don't got what yours does: the ice. *(Comet exits. Prix stares thoughtfully after Comet awhile, then opens the bag and pulls out the new vials. Silently counts.)*

Scene 2

Prison cell. Prix and Denise in prison uniforms. Denise putting sponge rollers in her hair. Prix lying supine on her upper bunk staring at the ceiling. A personal letter out of its envelope lies flat on her belly.

DENISE. Four years we been together, I assumin' you got nary a friend in the world. Then ha ha, joke on me: here come a letter.

That the first you had since you been in, right? *(No answer.)* I seen the return. 'Nother prison. But can't be nothin' too excitin', no big deals bein' made cuz sure thing they tore 'at sucker open, read it, must be personal, I heard you's all alone in the world, who you got personal? *(No answer.)* How come you got no kids? How ol' you, twenty-eight? By the time I was twenty-eight I had six and pregnant with number seven. I heard 'boutchu. I know 'boutchu but the rumors conflict. You been with it all, men, women, dogs. Flip side: never been touched. Which? *(No answer.)* Come on! I got a cigarette bet on the former. Betchu lost your virginity early in the day, how ol'? Thirteen? Twelve?

PRIX. *(Dry.)* Five.

DENISE. *Yes!* Terror terror. You was one of 'em, right? I done a little damage my day but you was a biggie I hear. Pre-eighteen but you knew when to stop. Get the hardcore felonies erased, your permanent record. You be out soon, three years, right? Three be gone 'fore ya know it. I ain't even be parole eligible for at least next five.

PRIX. Two. *(Denise puzzled.)* My sentence was six. Served four years I be out two.

DENISE. See! no time. My steady assignment was undercover, fool the white people, let the ATM people feel safe, thinkin' this white girl in with 'em. "Just don't open your mouth, Paley," what my girls call me, "don't open your mouth 'til you pull the knife cuz soon's you part them pink lips your cover be blown: projects all over!" *(Guffaws.)*

PRIX. *(As Denise laughs.)* You *are* white.

DENISE. How I be white, onliest white people I ever see is TV. Teachers. Fifth grade bus trip to the museum. Might be born white how I stay white no role models. *(Beat.)* I don't mean to be in your business but I couldn't help but notice the return: same last name. *(Long pause.)*

PRIX. Mother. Junkie. Started in jail I guess Never touched it when I knew her.

DENISE. When you knew her?

PRIX. Last time … sixteen.

DENISE. You was *sixteen*? Ain't seen her *twelve years*? *(No answer.)* She wrote to tell you she's a junkie?

PRIX. Wrote to tell me AIDS. Early release. Pro bono.

DENISE. *(Pause.)* Not me. Not my kids, whatever happens ... Every Tuesday I see 'em, once a month my mother, we stickin' it out, the family ties we — *(Sudden teenage laughter, rowdiness, in the corridor. Denise rushes to the bars to see. After they have passed and it is quiet again:)* I like the Ladies' groups. You like 'em? The counselin', classes. I missed my eight-thirty readin' class this mornin' and sat in on the adolescents' ten o'clock to make up. Rowdy! Forgot how rowdy they get, way *we* was SO glad not to be around that no more, so glad not to *be* that no more. Least Ladies got *some* kinda respect, 'preciate we know how to be: polite to each other, quiet to each other. With them two new ones now we got nine, nine's a good group.

PRIX. Eight.

DENISE. Aintchu precise with the numbers today! Too bad you weren't so quick when ya screwed up the codes yesterday breakfast. *(Pause.)*

PRIX. *What?*

DENISE. I heard that girl servin' the slop take your tray, tap it three times, plop the scrambled eggs your plate, tap the tray seven times. Three *seven*. Then I heardja pass by that other bitch and out the side a your mouth, "Thirty-*eight*." *(Prix stares at her.)*

PRIX. She tapped eight times!

DENISE. I could see where you could make the mistake. She did somethin', took a little breath space between third and fourth taps and your mind accidentally filled in the extra. *(Prix stunned, confused. Then looks at Denise, about to protest.)* Yeah. I'm sure.

PRIX. *(Incredulous.)* She fucked me up. She fucked me up!

DENISE. Ain't the first time this month neither. Messin' up, tell ya, I useta be in it but when my babies startin' comin', re*tire*. And gettin' into a fuckup habit's one sure sign you bes' do the same.

PRIX. Wait. That deal went down yesterday afternoon. I seen her yesterday evenin'. You're the one that's fucked up, if I'm screwed I'da sure knowed it by now.

DENISE. You're screwed. I overheard. She just waitin' for the moment.

PRIX. How do you know? *(Denise doesn't answer. Prix yanks Denise's head back.)* How do you know?

DENISE. I just heard it! I ain't with nobody no more! *(Prix still*

33

holds Denise's head back a few moments, then lets go.) That's the point. On the outside lookin' in, comfy chair. Sit back, watch the sparks fly without bein' one of 'em. From my viewpoint, I can predict it all.
PRIX. She's gonna kill me, fuck.
DENISE. Predicted you'd mess up. When I was in it, thirty-seven meant shipment pickup in the laundry room, thirty-eight the gym. Guess things changed by now?
PRIX. She's gonna kill me! fuck!
DENISE. You been in it too long, in it too long ya lose it. O.G. everybody want it. O.G. Original Gangsta, shit. You earned that years ago, what you stick around for? Ain't twenty-eight bit old for the gangs? *(Hair:)* I'm gonna cut all this shit off. My hair get curlier when it's close, and them close cuts all sophistication. *(Pause.)* When you said you was gonna make a fireworks show. You serious? *(No answer.)* I sure as hell couldn't. Set a thing up, then see one a them hot sparks fly off, come fallin' down right on top a ya *no! (Pause.)*
PRIX. Scariest is the opposite. Black shell. Send it up and somethin' go wrong: it don't explode. And in the blacka night, you can't see where it's fallin'. You know that live explosive's on the way back down, right down to ya. You just can't see where it's comin' from.

Scene 3

Denise sits on a bench smoking, watching Socks push a broom. Denise's broom stands idle against the wall near her. Socks is bent and grey, her face rarely visible since she doesn't look into others' eyes. She has some teeth missing and gives the impression of a person who has aged too quickly, who is really much younger than she appears. She speaks to no one in particular.

SOCKS. I useta have kids. I had three and the welfare took two, I can't remember what happen to that other boy. His daddy! that's what, motherfucker fought for him then wouldn't let me come close. Yaw, shit! yaw should get a goddamn vacuum cleaner, how

this thing s'posed to clean up all this shit? Damn, how many straws left in this fuckin' thing, three? Daddy, his goddamn motherfucker daddy took him. What was that motherfucker's name?
C.O. *(Off:)* Get to work, Denise!
DENISE. *(Mumbling to herself:)* I ain't workin' with that ol' crackhead, you must be outa your damn —
C.O. WORK! *(Denise, pissed, lazily pushes the broom, no rhyme or reason.)*

DENISE.	SOCKS.
	Remember, runnin' he ram that
My shift over five minutes	nail up his foot? You say "We
What's the goddamn point I	take it out It be fine" Bullshit!
start now? *hate* this fuckin	I know what to do — emergency
job! hate workin' with fuckin'	room: tetanus. What planet
addicts and AIDS	you on?

DENISE. *(Louder:)* Shit, Socks, you're sweepin' your goddamn dust on my toes! *(Prix enters.)* Glad you're here, relieve me, nothin' round here but fuckin' addicts and AIDS. *(Prix takes Denise's broom, starts sweeping, ignores Denise.)* Aintchu lucky you got switched out the kitchen. This nuthouse crackhead, and guess who I was stuck with before her? *Socks! you sweep shit on my feet again I lay you out!* Some dumb ol' smack bitch, done the needle once too much now got the full-blown, this ain't a penal colony, it's a leper colony. *(Starts to leave.)*
C.O. *(Off:)* Stay there, Denise.
DENISE. *What?*
C.O. *Stay there.*
DENISE. Shit! what is it now. Guess I ain't worked hard enough for 'em guess they expect me to do some other goddamn job, I ain't no goddamn slave. *(Sits. Beat.)* You know two a the counselors quit. Just like the six others this year 'cept they ain't found a replacement yet, this means tomorrow's counselin' group got the goddamn adolescents mixed in, our nice quiet adult session have present the damn disruptin' brats.
C.O. *(Off:)* Toilet cleanin'.
DENISE. *(To C.O., incredulous:)* Who? *(Gets the answer.)* Fuck! Fuck fuck fuck! *(Denise exits. Socks and Prix push brooms in silence awhile. Eventually Prix absently sweeps near Socks.)*

SOCKS. Outa here! Outa here! that's your place here's mine, I ain't come close to you You don't come close to me! Space! *(Socks goes back to work, sweeping more rapidly than before. Prix stares at her, stunned.)* PRIX. Malika? *(Malika [Socks] instantly stops pushing the broom, stares at Prix, terrified. Silence.)* Prix. *(Malika continues to stare at Prix, confused as to what to do.)*

MALIKA. I gotta go to the bathroom. *(Pause.)* I GOTTA GO TO THE BATHROOM! I GOTTA GO TO THE BATHROOM! I GOTTA GO TO THE BATHROOM! I GOTTA GO —

C.O. *(Entering.)* Okay, Socks, shut up! *(C.O. snatches Malika's arm and starts to escort her off but Malika pulls back.)* Hey! *(Malika hesitantly touches the C.O.'s metal name pin, sees her reflection in it. Glances in Prix's direction without looking directly at Prix. Exits with C.O.)*

Scene 4

The table with partition from Act One, Scene 3, this time Mother on the visitors' side. A C.O. nearby. Mother may appear a bit ill but has tried to look her best, perhaps overdoing the makeup a smidge. An uncomfortably long silence. Eventually Mother, tense, pulls out a compact mirror, checks her lipstick. The C.O. glances at her watch. Mother instantly jumps, snaps. Throughout Mother's speech the C.O. is unmoved.

MOTHER. Made up your mind, right? She's not comin' right who ast ya? Time, she got 'til five so shut it! Shut up all your comments, judgments, judge me *nerve!* Some nerve you got dontchu *dare* label me, us you know nothin' you think Well how long she gonna sit? She been here since starta visitin' hours one P.M. don't she gotta go to the bathroom? I stay here 'til five I haveta, which is all I ast a you, tell me when it's five *(C.O. looks at watch.)* no other reason you need to open your mouth, snortin' like you got it all figured out, our relationship, mother-daughter, nuuna your biz—

C.O. *Five. (Mother startled. Gathers her mirror, lipstick, purse. Exits.)*

Scene 5

*Prix using the bathroom, her feet visible beneath. Two
teenage girls enter, get in line for the bathroom. Prix in
prison garb, the girls in street clothes.*

PEPPER. She's all snotty, like, "No one should be in here for parole
violation." I'm like "Mrs. Garcia, I couldn't help it." She's like,
"That's stupid, Pepper, all you had to do was show up four o'clock
like you s'posed ta." I'm like "Bitch, you *know* where the goddamn
juvenile office is *Told* ja I be crossin' lines get myself killed," she's like,
"Thought you weren't in it no more." How stupid is she? Like just
cuz I decide to quit today the enemy conveniently get amnesia, don't
remember last week I was gang? Shit.
GIRL. She just ain't gettin' it regular. *(Both girls giggle.)*
PEPPER. Fuck, you always say that.
GIRL. The other day fiddlin' with her purse I saw her pull out a
condom. She put it back real fast hopin' no one noticed.
PEPPER. If she carryin' protection around I guess she gettin' it
regular.
GIRL. Women gettin' it regular has their men carryin' it around.
Woman gotta carry it herself just hopin' for a accidental emergency.
(They're laughing bigger.) She know I saw too, I saw the look —
*(Jupiter enters: Pepper and the girl immediately fall to silence, not look-
ing at each other. The door opens: Prix sees Jupiter. Jupiter gives Pepper
and the girl a look. They push Prix back into the stall, slamming the
door behind them. Sound: Pepper and the girl punching and kicking
the crap out of Prix. Jupiter, keeping watch outside, finally opens the
door, allowing the audience to see: Prix being beaten severely.)*
JUPITER. Okay. *(The violence ceases.)* Liked your speech. *(The
girls giggle.)*
PRIX. *(Struggling to speak.)* You didn't like it.
JUPITER. Pulled the heart, teared the eye. *(Long e in "teared."
Prix mumbles.)*

JUPITER. WHAT?

PRIX. *(Still struggling against the pain:)* Ancient. Years ago I wrote it, today remembered ... few words, today ... matters.

JUPITER. Matters to who? Pile a shit The Ladies liked it. The Ladies listen like you the prize poet Ladies The Ladies how the fuck old are ya ole ladies? Thirty?

PRIX. Twenty-eight.

JUPITER. Speak, Twenty-eight.

PRIX. You're fourteen. I came to your christenin'. *(Jupiter violently raises Prix to her knees.)*

JUPITER. Speak!

PRIX. *(On her knees.)* The accepting, nonjudgmental atmosphere of my group has allowed me to reevaluate my choices. ... helped me to see my errors attributable to ... to upbringing as well as personal choice sometimes ... Sometimes I think if I had been shown one kindness ... *(Prix stops. Pepper and the Girl, who had been rolling on the floor, gales of laughter, become quiet when they realize Prix has stopped.)*

GIRL. You didn't finish it.

PEPPER. *(More eager than unkind:)* Say the best part. Say it! *(Prix gathers her strength.)*

PRIX. On this day ... we are sisters — *(The girls whoop it up.)*

PEPPER and GIRL. "My sisters" "My sisters"! *(Jupiter stares at Prix as the other girls roar.)*

JUPITER. You say that so fuckin' serious like you believe that crap. *(Long pause.)*

PRIX. I don't.

JUPITER. *(Eyes still on Prix.)* Get the fuck outa here. *(Pepper and the Girl confused. Jupiter glares at them. They exit quick.)*

PEPPER. Sorry, Jupiter.

JUPITER. Get up. *(Prix does.)* Usually I ain't s' hands off, don't order no one kick the shit outa someone without I'm right there in with 'em, but doctor said I gotta watch the physical stuff. First trimester.

PRIX. Sorry, Jupit — *(Jupiter snaps open the toilet, puts Prix's head in and flushes several times. Snaps Prix's head out and immediately pulls a razor from her own mouth, puts it against Prix's throat. Choking.)* Your mother ... Your mother —

JUPITER. My mother fuck! Like I ever see the bitch between jail

38

and the fosters *good!* And each time I'm took away she wanna bawl and bawl like she so Christ fuckin' sad fuck her! Dontcha be mentionin' her fuckin' stupid name to me Don't be bringin' up no goddamn Comet!

PRIX. Your third birthday, she show me the shoppin' bag. Pooh bear. *(Jupiter glaring at Prix. Then suddenly slams Prix's head against the back of the toilet.)*

JUPITER. Original Gangsta. *(Jupiter exits laughing.)*

Scene 6

Picnic table. Angel clears the remnants of dinner. A pattern that repeats every few seconds: Prix looking into the sky, Angel looking at her watch, Prix looking at her watch.

ANGEL. Few broken ribs. There was this blod clot, scared us awhile but then it cleared up. Told us they figure he be released Tuesday. *(To kids in distance:)* LET GO A HIM! HEY, HE WOULDN'TA BEEN DOIN' IT TO YOU IF YOU WEREN'T DOIN' IT TO HIM FIRST! And they still chargin' him, resistin' arrest, how the fuck when they ain't got a scratch and his body covered in blood? shit. I don't know why he don't get ridda that damn car anyway, he been stopped harrassed three times in four months ain't he figured out yet cops don't like a black man drivin' that make a car? GET DOWN! I TOLDJA STAY OUTA THAT DAMN TREE! Guess your parole officer set you up, some real excitin' job.

PRIX. Burger King.

ANGEL. He ain't like you and me, my brothers ... Like Vince, total innocent, football, *A*s and *B*s then walk into them drive-by bullets. And Darryl. Darryl ain't done a wrong thing his whole life, nothin' but take care a his girlfriend his kids, which what sent him to jail first time. Illegal sale a food stamps ooh ain't they cheatin' on the taxpayers, ain't the taxpayers so mad he cheated thirty

39

bucks this month feed his kids while business people writin' off two hundred dollar lunches every fuckin' day a the week but yeah, taxpayers pay that, that's fine, that's legal.

PRIX. Clear night.

ANGEL. Worst is sentenced him to lifetime a welfare, every time my baby brother try for employment, can't get past the application question: "You ever been convicted of a felony?" Why you keep lookin' at your watch?!

PRIX. Why you?

ANGEL. Somethin' up my sleeve *told* ja! Surprise! *(Prix: vague snicker. Then:)*

PRIX. When?

ANGEL. Dontchu worry about it I'll letcha know. When it's ready I'll letcha know. My question: what train you got to catch?

PRIX. *(Beat.)* Daily check-in. She said she be in the neighborhood on the hour *don't be late.* If I get sent back sure ain't be cuza violation a parole.

ANGEL. My plans!

PRIX. Won't take more 'n a minute I ain't leavin'. *(Mutter-chuckle:)* Plans. *(Beat.)*

ANGEL. Run into Comet the other day, supermarket. Big as a house. Invite me to her baby shower, Sunday. Wanna go? *(For the first time Prix looks right at Angel.)*

PRIX. I ain't never in my life uttered a kind syllable to Comet now why you think she want me at her shower?

ANGEL. You useta go to that shit. "Free cake" you say.

PRIX. Only invited cuz a office politics, me her boss. Then. *(Beat.)* Why you invite me to this? Your oldest fourth grade and I ain't never bothered to meet none of 'em 'til today I ain't exactly close family.

ANGEL. Third grade. My mother thought it be nice to ask, havin' the picnic anyway why not make it a Welcome Home Prix. She called to work, your moms not feelin' well, all this food ... *(Beat.)* Didn't expect ya to accept. *(Chuckles.)* First you don't. "Prix, you liketa come?" "No." Thirty seconds you call back, "Yes. I'll bring some chocolate chips." Why you change your mind?

PRIX. I dunno. Five weeks outa jail, somethin' to do 'sides work. TV.

ANGEL. *(Beat.)* Nice, delayin' things this year. Quiet. We in this spot every Fourth GIVE IT BACK! and the park wall-to-wall packed. Not all bad the kids chicken pox in bed over the holiday, here we are now, space and peace. *(Angel takes out a photograph, hands it to Prix.)* Happy Twenty-sixth a July. *(Prix studies the photo.)*

PRIX. Where was *this?*

ANGEL. Our old old apartment. Don't remember it? *(Prix shakes her head no.)* We were six, first grade. Sonia was seven, Darryl three. And Vince! All us standin' fronta the tree like we told but big brother, Mr. Independent, gotta be on the bike.

PRIX. I remember those decorations. Yaw ever buy any new ones? Same ol' glitter bell, same ol' star. 'Cept ... looks so new. *(Chuckles.)* Darryl! That baby grin, people always tellin' babies to smile, only thing they know how to do is show their teeth and grit 'em.

ANGEL. Like your smile was any realer. Prix the Sad Sack, even if we freeze tag even if we double-dutch you one a them kids always got somethin' unhappy behind all the giggle-play. *(Prix studies the picture more closely.)*

PRIX. I'm smilin'.

ANGEL. Look at it. *(Prix studies the picture again. Now she sees it and, as best she can, suppresses the sudden, painful memory. Then looks at her watch.)*

PRIX. Time. *(Prix snatches her empty backpack, looping it on one shoulder, and quickly gets up to leave.)*

ANGEL. I *knew* it! I *knew* it!

PRIX. What?

ANGEL. *(Clutching part of the backpack.)* You makin' a connection! Month out and already you back. Not around my kids! I left it years ago, Prix, I grew up!

PRIX. *(Mutters as she exits.)* You don't know what you're talkin' about.

ANGEL. *(Calling:)* Don't I? *I* learned somethin'! *I* learned somethin'! *(Angel starts clearing table again, slamming stuff.)* COME ON, YAW, WE LEAVIN'! *(Angel continues clearing. Then, aware the kids have ignored her:)* COME ON! *(Prix returns with a stuffed backpack. Angel sees.)* Fuck you, Prix! I don't *know* you Ain't settin' *me* up guilt by association GO! Bring that shit around my kids COME ON! Fuck you! Fuck you! Fuck — *(Prix has unzipped the bag for Angel to peer in. Angel does, and is surprised. Prix pulls out a rocket, touching it tenderly.)*

PRIX. I got it planned. This ain't the big show I always wanted, Class B, but I do okay with these home 'works, aerials and fountains and roman candles, rockets, still meticulous with the color effects, style. Whole show won't be five minutes, I could drag it out make it last and everyone waitin', waitin anticipatin' the next shell but the excitement, the euphoria is in the momentum don't drop it. I paint the emotional rhythms, some calmer than others these peaks and dips important to prevent monotony, just never let drop the thrill to nil. *(Angel, fascinated, has pulled out a few of the fireworks, looking them over.)*

ANGEL. My kids regret I call they pay me no mine when I tell 'em what they missed. *(Still fascinated. Then:)* Hey! These can't explode by touch can they? My hands kinda hot and sweaty ain't gonna light no fuse, right? Mushroom cloud?

PRIX. When it's over ... You ever see what it's like, enda the big Fourth show, East River? Two types a people. First is the two million who seen it, walkin' in a daze a beauty high. Harmony. Second is the people in the cars waitin' for the harmony heads-in-the-clouds people to cross the damn street, beepin' and all fury, impatient anyway but now hoppin' mad cuz they confused: How come pedestrians ain't gettin' mad right back? Cuz just when we thought couldn't get no more radiant no more splenderous than it already has it does, sometimes so high I wish it *would* stop, I think can't nobody stand this much ... beauty? No. Ecstasy. *(Prix studies the sky. Then looks at Angel.)* Stand back. *(Angel exits. Prix walks around a bit, anxious, preparing herself. Then stoops. Lights a match. The fireworks. Prix stares. Elation. Sound: slow squeaky wheels. Prix turns to look offstage to the approaching sound. Jo enters in a squeaky wheelchair. Slowly turning. Prix stares at her.)*

JO. You done it. *(Prix smiles. Then sees Jo's eyes, looks at the wheelchair. It dawns on her. Prix begins shaking her head.)*

PRIX. No ...

JO. YOU DONE IT!

PRIX. NO! Done what? I don't know you!

JO. You know me.

PRIX. Don't!

JO. YES!

JO'S FRIEND. *(Entering.)* C'mon, Jo.

JO. She says she don't know me!

JO'S FRIEND. She knows you.

PRIX. *I don't!*

JO'S FRIEND. *Bitch!* she knows! *(Prix vehemently shaking her head.)*

JO. You sixteen, me seventeen, the zoo. *(Prix blank.)* BRONX ZOO! REPTILES!

PRIX. I DON'T REMEMBER!

JO. She says she don't remember! *(By now, Angel has entered.)*

JO'S FRIEND. Fucker!

PRIX. I don't know, I don't —

JO. She don't remember!

JO'S FRIEND. BITCH!

PRIX. It mighta happened! I ain't sayin' it didn't happen, a lotta stuff ... Long time ago, lotta stuff blur I don't remember it all! Lotta stuff I did Don't remember it all! *(Friend is wheeling Jo off.)* DON'T REMEMBER IT ALL! *(Just before Friend gets Jo off, Jo pushes Friend's hands away and, with great effort, turns 360 degrees around to face Prix. She stares at Prix a long time, and Prix stares back until she can't stand it, looks away.)*

JO. This ain't the half of it. *(Jo turns back around, wheels herself off, accompanied by Friend. Prix stares where they exited, then swings around to Angel.)*

PRIX. I don't remember her! *(Angel says nothing.)* You know her? I don't! I don't remember her! *(Angel says nothing.)* It ain't s'posed to be like this! It ain't ... if we had differences, gone! Gone, you ever see the Fourth, East River? *Every*body's happy, everybody, no anger! No anger! *(Beat.)* I didn't do 'em right. Maybe I done 'em wrong musta put the wrong colors together, clashed some colors dampered the emotional scheme WHAT'D I DO? *(Pause.)*

ANGEL. It's time. Come on.

PRIX. You remember her? *(Angel shakes her head no.)* I know! I had two greens together, too much repetition too much cool. I fucked it up.

ANGEL. Maybe she just crazy. *(Prix turns to Angel quickly, this suggestion having given her great hope. Just as quickly she is disappointed to see in Angel's face that Angel doesn't believe what she just said. Turns back to stare in the direction Jo exited.)*

PRIX. I ain't callin' her a liar just ... *(Pause.)*

43

ANGEL. *(Exiting.)* It's time. Come on. *(Prix continues to stare after Jo. Finally she turns around. Angel is gone. Confused, she looks for Angel in the dark. In a narrow space, Prix is startled to find Angel and a hugely pregnant Comet.)*
PRIX. Comet … *(Comet gives Angel a look. Prix, suddenly feeling surrounded and terrified, gives an unconscious cry, backing up. Comet and Angel pull out from behind their backs several of Prix's colored pen lights and form fireworks for Prix. Prix suppresses her sobs.)*

Scene 7

Thirty-Fourth Street and Fifth Avenue. Prix's mother, tired, weak, on the corner. The lights of the city reflect upon her — particularly, because she stands right in front of it, the blue and yellow of the Empire State Building. Prix enters. Her voice is flat, expressionless. If she has worried at all about her mother, she conceals it well.)

PRIX. What.
MOTHER. *(Pleased:)* Found me! *(The effort to speak sends her into a coughing fit.)*
PRIX. Your goddamn note was pretty specific, Thirty-Fourth and Fifth. Half expected to see your guts splattered where you're standin' why the hell else you be at the Empire State Buildin' midnight.
MOTHER. *Almost* midnight. Remember? *(Prix stares at her, still expressionless.)* Lights out! Midnight, they turn off the Empire State.
PRIX. You come all the way down here for that. *(Mother grins.)* Let's go. *(Turns to leave.)*
MOTHER. *NO!* Wantchu to see.
PRIX. I believe you, come on.
MOTHER. You don't believe me.
PRIX. If ya gone to all the trouble a comin' down here to prove it must be true. Come on, we'll watch it on the way to the subway, you know they space the trains half-hour apart after twelve. *(Mother won't*

44

budge.) They got me on the goddamn breakfast shift I gotta be there goddamn five A.M. prepare the goddamn powdered eggs and biscuits. We leave now and if the odds with us, no wait for the train, maybe we make it home by one, maybe I get a luxury three hours' sleep.

MOTHER. I hate they give you that job! That's parole board's idea a keepin' you outa jail, can't support yourself plus they know you got me, how they speck you to survive?

PRIX. *(More to herself.)* I found a little supplemental income. *(Mother scared.)* Don't flip I ain't in it no more just here and there: sell a few food stamps, bitta herb. Don't freak. Retired. Thirty pretty old to still bang in the gangs. *(Beat.)* How much longer?

MOTHER. Seconds. *(Prix, hands in jacket pockets, leans against a pole.)* What day's today? I mean, what's blue and yellow?

PRIX. Nothin'.

MOTHER. Somethin'.

PRIX. Nothin'. Red Valentine's, red and green Christmas, red white and blue Fourth, people start assumin' every Empire State color combo means somethin'. 'S arbitrary, every day ain't a holiday but Empire still gotta be lit.

MOTHER. 'Til midnight. *(Pause.)* You ever thinka him?

PRIX. Who? *(Mother looks at Prix. Now Prix understands who Mother means and is startled as she realizes she hasn't thought of him.)* No. No, useta. Useta think about him all the time. Not lately. Not in years. *(Pause.)*

MOTHER. Different. Was a time you'da seen that note from me, tossed it in the trash, gone boutcher business. Seems you different all growed up, seems you ain't s' mad no more. *(Prix says nothing.)* These colors. They nice together? *(Prix studies them.)*

PRIX. Blue and yellow, cool and warm. Sweet. Fireworks, blue's hardest color to mix.

MOTHER. Shoot. Nursin' a little bitta flu, 'f I'da known boutcher fireworks show … *(Beat.)*

PRIX. Didn't work out. Think I keep it a spectator sport from now on.

MOTHER. We go to the fireworks, I can't hardly look at 'em. Busy starin' at your face. The wonder, happy happy. And best is when it's over, after the last big boom the moment the lights all out, I see in your eyes a … sweetness. Calm after the joy storm.

45

(The sixteen-note church-bell hour tune begins, followed by the twelve tolls. Soon after the tune starts, Prix speaks:)

PRIX. Midnight.

MOTHER. Wait. *(They watch in silence a few moments.)* Prix. What happen to all your artwork? Fireworks things.

PRIX. Angel saved the pen lights. Rest got lost or thrown out while I was in jail.

MOTHER. Them figures? Pipe cleaners?

PRIX. Gone.

MOTHER. Useta always be new ones, you constant recreatin'. How come you ain't replaced 'em? I don't ever see ya doin' your sketches no more, that was your one thing, one thing hope you ain't lost interest. *(Prix says nothing.)* I wisht I'da kept one. Wisht you still made 'em pipe cleaner figures I wisht I had one for me. *(Pause.)* Prix. I know … I know you ain't much into grantin' favors but … *(Pulls much change from her pocket.)* I found some money today, I thought —

PRIX. I toldju not to do that! Panhandlin', Jesus! we ain't fuckin' beggars!

MOTHER. I just thought, maybe you can't afford the pipe cleaners, maybe that why you don't do it no more.

PRIX. Do I look like I got time to fool around, arts and crafts? Grown woman. *(Beat. Then Mother holds out coins to Prix.)*

MOTHER. Prix. You make one? For me? *(Prix, pointedly looking at the building and not at her mother, shakes her head no. Mother stares. Then, sudden and desperate:)* PRIX! YOU MAKE ONE? FOR ME? *(The force of her emotion causes Mother to drop her coins. She falls to her knees to pick them up. Prix starts to help but Mother violently waves her away. Prix gazes at her mother, for the first time in the play really seeing her. Mother gathers most of the money, then stops. Just after the twelfth bell toll [the elongated reverberations or increased volume should indicate its finality], Mother lifts her face to look at Prix.)*

PRIX. Yes. *(The lights of the Empire State Building go out.)*

End of Play

PROPERTY LIST

Colored pencils, drawings, drawing pad (PRIX)
Pencil with eraser, notepad (PRIX)
Hair extensions (ANGEL)
Phone (PRIX)
Pipe cleaners and pipe-cleaner figures (PRIX)
Razor blade (COMET, PRIX, JUPITER)
Pen lights (PRIX, ANGEL, COMET)
Desk lamp (PRIX)
Paper clip (JEROME)
Glue stick, newspaper clippings, scrapbook (ANGEL)
Wristwatches (ANGEL, PRIX)
Crocheted gloves (MOTHER)
Cloth hairband (CAT)
Bedsheet (CAT)
Tattered paperback — black romance novel (PRIX)
Coffee (JEROME)
Milkshake (PRIX)
Clock-radio, gun (PRIX)
Crack vials (PRIX)
Cupcake with dynamite candle (PRIX)
Backpack — full, then empty (PRIX)
Sponge rollers for hair (DENISE)
Letter and envelope (PRIX)
Brooms (DENISE, SOCKS)
Lit cigarette (DENISE)
Metal nametag (C.O.)
Purse, compact, lipstick (MOTHER)
Picnic remnants (ANGEL)
Photograph (ANGEL)
Rocket, fireworks, matches (PRIX)
Wheelchair (JO)
Coins (MOTHER)

SOUND EFFECTS

Fireworks
Phone ringing
Knock on door
Man and woman laughing, sexual breathing
Sounds of a violent fight, furniture banging
Toilet flushing
Jiggling doorknob
Weeping
Tapping on wall
Radio
Teenage laughter
Slow, squeaky wheels
Church bell 16-note song, followed by 12 tolls